I Want
You to Be Happy

Other books by

Blue Mountain Press INC

Come Into the Mountains, Dear Friend
by Susan Polis Schutz
I Want to Laugh, I Want to Cry
by Susan Polis Schutz
Peace Flows from the Sky
by Susan Polis Schutz
Someone Else to Love
by Susan Polis Schutz
I'm Not That Kind of Girl
by Susan Polis Schutz
Yours If You Ask
by Susan Polis Schutz
The Best Is Yet to Be
Step to the Music You Hear, Vol. I
The Language of Friendship
The Language of Love
The Language of Happiness
The Desiderata of Happiness
by Max Ehrmann
Whatever Is, Is Best
by Ella Wheeler Wilcox
Poor Richard's Quotations
by Benjamin Franklin
I Care About Your Happiness
by Kahlil Gibran/Mary Haskell
My Life and Love Are One
by Vincent Van Gogh
I Wish You Good Spaces
by Gordon Lightfoot
We Are All Children Searching for Love
by Leonard Nimoy
Come Be with Me
by Leonard Nimoy
Catch Me with Your Smile
by Peter McWilliams
Creeds to Love and Live By
On the Wings of Friendship
Think of Me Kindly
by Ludwig van Beethoven
You've Got a Friend
Carole King

I Want You to Be Happy

Selections from the songs and drawings of

Hoyt Axton

Edited by Susan Polis Schutz

Blue Mountain Press T.M.

Boulder, Colorado

Library of Congress Number: 78-65230
ISBN: 0-88396-039-7

Manufactured in the United States of America

First Printing: January, 1979

Acknowledgments are on pages 62-63

Blue Mountain Press INC.

P.O. Box 4549, Boulder, Colorado 80306

CONTENTS

*Someone once told me in a dream
that truth was a great white bird.
Here are some feathers I found.*

Hoyt Axton

About the Author

Hoyt Axton recognizes the beauty and wonder of lif
shares his joyous vision with the world. "My philosophy
the positive," says Hoyt, "and I try to live by that." Wl
noted for his songwriting skills, he is also successfu
artist, actor, poet and performer. Hoyt feels that musi
language," and that music is the "best way of getting pec
going together."

This talent for translating the pulse of the world intc
resulted in 18 record albums and many hit songs, inclu
Greenback Dollar, Boney Fingers, Never Been to Spa

Morning Comes, The No No Song and the truly classic *Joy to the World*. A measure of Hoyt's popularity is reflected in the number of people who have recorded his songs, including Joan Baez, Elvis Presley, Cher, John Denver, Helen Reddy, Ringo Starr and Arlo Guthrie.

Hoyt's special appeal stems from the influence of song-loving parents and from the many musical styles he has experienced while moving from Oklahoma to Florida and finally to California. It is this eclectic background that has made Hoyt into a singer-songwriter who defies categorization. While sometimes country, sometimes rock and sometimes folk, Hoyt's songs continually speak a "universal language."

Come stand by my side
where I'm going
Take my hand
if I stumble and fall
It's the strength that you share
when you're growing
that gives me what I need
most of all

I'd like to live
I'd like to be
I'd like to give
all the giving in me

I am less
than the song I am singing
I am more
than I thought I could be
Spent some time
as a child in daydreaming
As a young man
I sailed on the sea

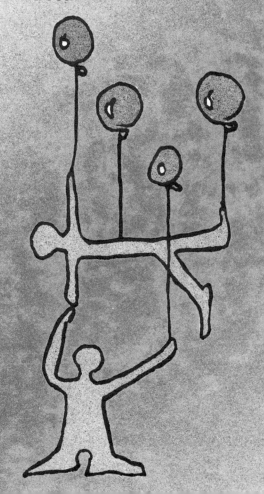

Different minds
different changes
different reasons to believe
Some far journeys we have taken
some sweet dreams we had to leave
And I want you to be happy
and I hope you always will
For I cannot rest easy
until all your dreams
are real

Unfold
your wings
and fly
away into
the starry sky . . .
Friend of mine
. . . have a good time

You find
that secret place
in your mind
where the light of
understanding love . . .
outshines the sun

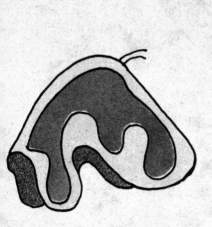

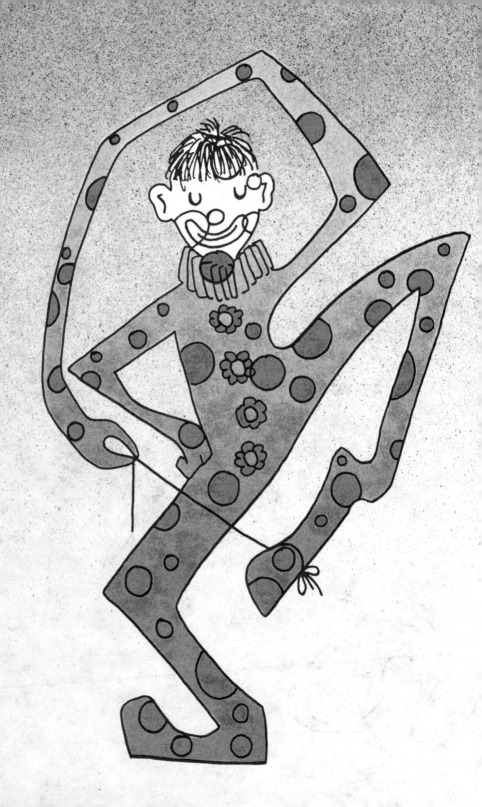

Looking for love
in the misty waters
of the seas that roll . . .

Do you believe in dreams?
Do you believe in dreamers?
I hope that you'll find
what you're looking for
You don't have to worry

There's a bright tomorrow in
. . . doing the best that you can
. . . looking for love

I'll never
treat you wrong
won't make you cry
just sing your sweet love song
won't tell you lies
Wouldn't you like
to go riding with me
into tomorrow
sweet fantasy

Do you remember
when we took a dream
and then turned
it
into
today together . . .

Cherish what you sweet remember
running through the sands of time
Cherish it with all
that's in you

Rivers will run
mountains will rise
I love you more
than the stars
in the skies
Rivers will run
eagles will fly
I love you more
than the stars
in the skies

I love you more
than the stars
in the skies

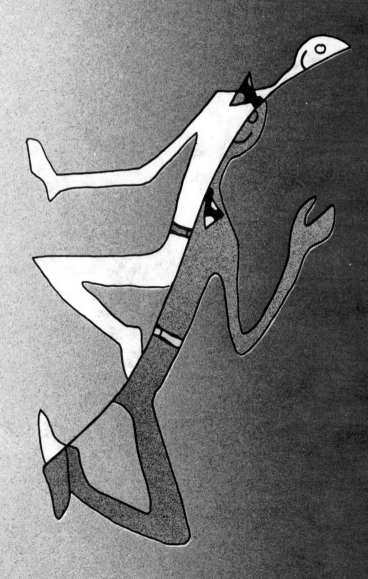

Though we
traveled different highways
our goals were the same . . .
singing songs
picking berries
running through the woods
having fun
making merry
doing now . . . as good

I love you

Your letter
seemed to carry me back
to where I want to be . . .

in your arms . . .
into tomorrow . . .
into today

together

The way we love
   is the way we live
And the way we sing
   is the way we give . . .

We're being
   who we are

Roses and moonlight
dancing on air
don't mean a thing
if you're not there –

walking beside me
living inside me

In dreams my memories ramble
where my heart cannot go
back to the love and the laughter . . .

How many nights did I want you
How many times did I try
You know you taught me to love you
Did you know you taught me how to cry

Sometimes I dream of the sky
You know who taught me to dream . . .
Did you know who taught me how to cry
And how many nights did I want you
How many times did I try
You know you taught me to love you
Did you know you taught me how to cry

I believe that somewhere
there are other starry skies . . .
I believe that somewhere
there are other happy days . . .
I believe that somewhere
there are other shining seas
where the rainbows are . . .

I'd like
to thank you
for standing
by me.

My dog had some puppies
Would you like to have one?
He will be your friend
and he will lick your face
He will never cheat you
He won't try to beat you
Help you be a winner
in the human race

Every
one
needs
a
friend.

31

I will
   . . . sail on a sea
   that's all my own
But I promise
I will write
when I am able
to understand the words
of a song sung far away
by a person with a voice
as soft as you . . .
   I bid you "adieu"
   . . . in the language of love

I'd like to help you
find someplace . . .
peace of mind

Leave all your pain behind
sail away free

33

True love
cannot be bought . . .
True love
cannot be borrowed
Just like a diamond
in a wishing well
It shines
beyond tomorrow

You are the object
   of my desire
You are the sun
   and the moon to me
And I believe
   in loving you . . .
You make me so happy . . .
I believe
   in loving you

Sometimes it's hard to write . . .
and find the words to rhyme to
Some people say you shouldn't
talk of love
unless you have the time to . . .

I just can't help it . . .
   I'm in love with you

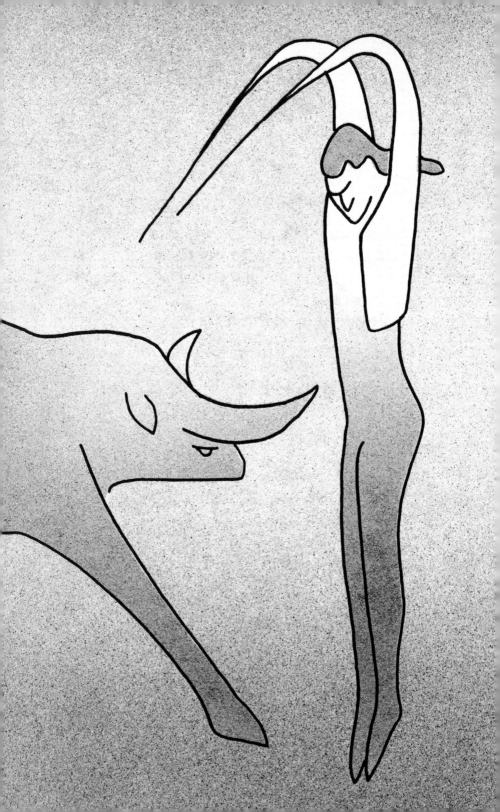

Do you remember
chasing a rainbow?
. . . dreaming dreams
. . . walking in the woods at night
. . . Can you remember the way
you were feeling?
Barefoot, running on a sunny day . . .

Try to remember the song
you were singing . . .
It made you happy
It kept you smiling

Try it again . . .
try it again

Heard you're feeling better
Glad you found some happy
In my time I've had
a little happy, too

If you let it get you up
you know I'll bet you
it will get you up
and keep you smiling through

Looking
for love
and understanding . . .
Just looking for
a smile
Trying to find
a little bit of laughter

Love's going to bring it
and we're going to sing it
and it's going to
be sweet

Summertime nights
are on my mind
And I wonder
how the folks are
back home
sweet home

If I could only
for one hour
be five years old
one more time . . .

But I have to come
to childhood's end
Said goodbye
to my toys and friends . . .
I know
I must grow up
someday
but I think
it will be
just like it was
in my childhood

Living and loving
and laughing
in the wildwood
living and running . . .
in the sun

Would you like to go
to Colorado?
Heaven is there
I'm told . . .
I'm leaving
in the morning
and I'd like to take
you with me . . .

Everything is real
in Colorado
Real is how you feel
in Colorado . . .
I'm tired of plastic people
with their neon souls aglow
So I'm going to try once more
in the mountains
Rocky Mountains

We could be happy
in the mountains
Everybody is talking
about the place
of their dreams
where they can find
peace of mind
I'm not sure
but I think it seems
I've finally found mine
in the mountains . . .

Up on the mountain
you don't need
your little blue pills . . .
You can leave
all the hang-ups
of the city
in the city
and the crystal morning sunshine
is so pretty
in the mountains . . .

Heaven is there

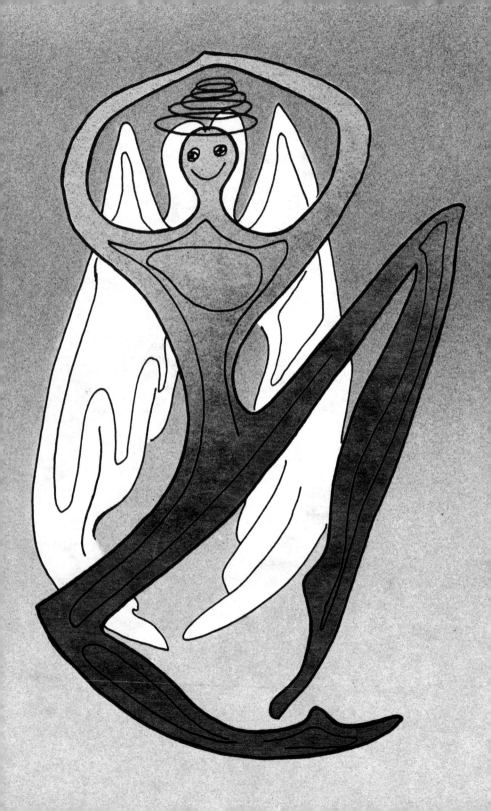

Sweet country days
the memories are clear
I'll remember the laughter . . .
I had when you
were here

I love your face
I love your quiet ways
If I could paint you in colors
you'd be a rainbow
in a summer day

When the world is wrong
. . . right yourself!
It will make the dark clouds fly . . .
Just don't let the spirit die
. . . be glad
when you see the dawn.

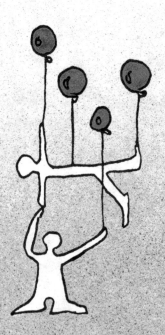

. . . Playgrounds
popcorn
and pink cotton candy
Disneyland daytimes
dance in the eyes
of freckle-faced, t-shirted
milk-drinking babies
who never have
ever seen
fire in the skies

And I hope
they never
will

I hope your sweet dreams
last forever . . .

Blessed is the dream
in which you live . . .
Holy is the taking
and the giving
of love

Everybody's working on
a great big life machine
Everybody's bound to have a story . . .

I believe in miracles . . .
I believe in the power
and the glory of dreaming
Sweet dreamer, dream on . . .
You put the wings
on the songs I sing
April, I love you . . .

Everybody wants to find
a ride up to heaven
nobody wants to make a climb
Heard you're giving lessons
teaching yourself to fly
You've got the wings
of a hummingbird

Love is going to get you by

Sweet dreamer
dream on . . .
I've been dreaming, too
nothing wrong with dreaming
sometimes
they come true !

Singing Joy
to the world
All
the boys and girls now
Joy
to the fishes
in the deep blue sea
Joy
to you
and me

I am the sea
and you are
a raging river

You are the sun
and I am
a crystal fountain
flowing in
the growing love
of living . . .

I am you
and you are me

When I first saw you,
    I first loved you
with a song
    that I sang . . .
    to your eyes.

Sometimes when I get lonely
I can swear
I hear you call
The nights are cold
when you don't keep me warm . . .
and sometimes I wonder
    if you think of me

Like a lion
in the winter
I can hear
the summer call
like a ship
out on the ocean
made of stone

And sometimes
when I get lonely
I can swear
I hear you call

When . . .
   you need some kind
   of helping hand
   to carry you through
I could ease your pain
   . . . I could lighten your load
   . . . I could make it
   just a little bit
   better for you

ACKNOWLEDGMENTS

"Come stand by my side," from the song *Less Than the Song*, by Hoyt Axton. Copyright © 1972 by Lady Jane Music.

"Different minds," from the song *Less Than the Song*, by Hoyt Axton. Copyright © 1972 by Lady Jane Music.

"Do you remember," from the song *Nothing to Lose*, by Hoyt Axton. Copyright © 1970 by Lady Jane Music.

"Everybody's working," from the song *Life Machine*, by Hoyt Axton. Copyright © 1973 by Lady Jane Music.

"Everyone," from the song *Paid in Advance*, by Hoyt Axton. Copyright © 1975 by Lady Jane Music.

"Heard you're feeling better," from the song *Sweet Misery*, by Hoyt Axton. Copyright © 1972 by Lady Jane Music.

"I am less than the song," from the song *Less Than the Song*, by Hoyt Axton. Copyright © 1972 by Lady Jane Music.

"I am the sea," from the song *Epistle*, by Hoyt Axton. Copyright © 1968, 1972 by Lady Jane Music.

"I believe that somewhere," from the song *Pride of Man*, by Hoyt Axton. Copyright © 1975 by Lady Jane Music.

"I hope your sweet dreams," from the song *Air Mail*, by Hoyt Axton. Copyright © 1971, 1972 by Lady Jane Music.

"I love you more," from the song *Sweet Fantasy*, by Hoyt Axton. Copyright © 1972 by Lady Jane Music.

"I'll never treat you wrong," from the song *Sweet Fantasy*, by Hoyt Axton. Copyright © 1972 by Lady Jane Music.

"I will sail," from the song *A Stone and a Feather*, by Hoyt Axton and Renee Armand. Copyright © 1976 by Lady Jane Music.

"I'd like to help you," from the song *Alice in Wonderland*, by Hoyt Axton. Copyright © 1970, 1972 by Lady Jane Music.

"I'd like to live," from the song *Alice in Wonderland*, by Hoyt Axton. Copyright © 1970, 1972 by Lady Jane Music.

"I'd like to thank you," from the song *Sweet Fantasy*, by Hoyt Axton. Copyright © 1972 by Lady Jane Music.

"If I could only," from the song *Childhood's End*, by Hoyt Axton. Copyright © 1968, 1972 by Lady Jane Music.

"In dreams my memories ramble," from the song *You Taught Me How to Cry*, by Hoyt Axton. Copyright © 1977 by Lady Jane Music.

"Like a lion in the winter," from the song *Lion in the Winter*, by Hoyt Axton. Copyright © 1974 by Lady Jane Music.

"Looking for love," from the song *In a Young Girl's Mind*, by Hoyt Axton and Mark Dawson. Copyright © 1974 by Lady Jane Music.

"Looking for love and understanding," from the song *Hungry Man* by Hoyt Axton. Copyright © 1972 by Lady Jane Music.

ACKNOWLEDGMENTS